Brookline Historical Publication Society

John White of Muddy River

.

Brookline Historical Publication Society

John White of Muddy River

ISBN/EAN: 9783744791564

Printed in Europe, USA, Canada, Australia, Japan

Cover: Foto ©ninafisch / pixelio.de

More available books at **www.hansebooks.com**

JOHN WHITE OF MUDDY RIVER

AND

DESCENDANTS OF HIS SON BENJAMIN.

Some four years ago Mr. Thomas J. Lothrop, then living
in this town, published a pamphlet entitled, John White of
Watertown and Brookline. It is a concise genealogical reg-
ister of five generations, under seventeen family heads with
117 children. At the present time there are living in the
town members of the 6th, 7th, 8th and 9th generations who
bear the family name, and of other names including the 10th.

The adult members of the second generation consisted of
three sons. The children of John White, Jr., the eldest
son, removed from Brookline and have not been associated
with Brookline history excepting Abigail, who married
William Sharp, and Sarah, who married John Winchester.

Descendants of the two younger sons have been citizens of
the town to the present day, and it may be said in a general
way, that those descended from Joseph, the second son, have
lived in the southern and western parts of the town centering
about what is now the junction of Warren and Heath streets,
while those descended from Benjamin, the youngest son, have
lived along the line of Washington street, either at the village
or near the southwest slope of Corey Hill and it is to this
division of the family that I shall confine myself.

Nothing is now known of John White, senior, before the
taking of the first inventory of estates at Watertown about
1639, when he is recorded as owner of a " Homestall and seven
acres of land" in that town. From the records of Suffolk
Deeds we learn that in 1642, Stephen Day mortgaged to John
White, seven acres of land and a house on the south side of
Charles River, and in the same year, Reinold Bush mortgaged
four acres also on the south side of the river ; while in 1643,
John White "deeds by way of mortgage to John Sherman, to
secure a debt of £25 due the heirs of the widow Ong, a house

and seven acres of land in Watertown bought from the Deacons, and a house and seven acres of land lying in Cambridge bought from Mr. Day."

As we first see him, thus dimly outlined in Watertown, he is probably twenty-six to thirty years of age and not long married. Tradition has it that his wife was Frances Scarboro, and it also tells us that his son Joseph married Hannah Scarboro, but I have, as yet, found no authentic record as to either. The given names of each of these early mothers of the Brookline Whites are well evidenced, but their family names are shrouded in the mists of the past.

The four children were born in Watertown, possibly excepting the youngest, Mary, who was baptized at Roxbury in 1652, "Mary daughter to sister White of Watertown," so the record runs.

Between the years 1636 and 1642, allotments of land at Muddy River, in various quantities, had been made to more than 100 persons, among whom the names of Aspinwall, Boylston, Griggs, Atkinson, Davis, Kenrick, Gross and others, are familiar to us at the present day. The bounds of these ancient grants are often quite obscure to any but the practised searcher. Fortunately some of them are more easy to trace.

Between Corey Hill and Aspinwall Hill, a small brook, following the general line of Washington and School streets and Aspinwall avenue, drains that valley, while between Aspinwall and Fisher Hills the larger brook drains the valley of the Circuit railway line.

Again the old boundary line separating from Roxbury was along the present "Village Lane" instead of the valley of Muddy River, in the Parkway. Let us now picture the land between the two brooks to an extent of two hundred and fifty acres. This was the grant to Mr. John Cotton.

A grant of 100 acres to Elder Thomas Leverett was bounded northerly by the brook separating his land from Mr. Cotton's, "the east end being a sharp angle."

A grant of 100 acres to Elder Thomas Oliver bordered Roxbury line on the south, and Mr. Leverett's land on the north, while the east end was also a sharp angle.

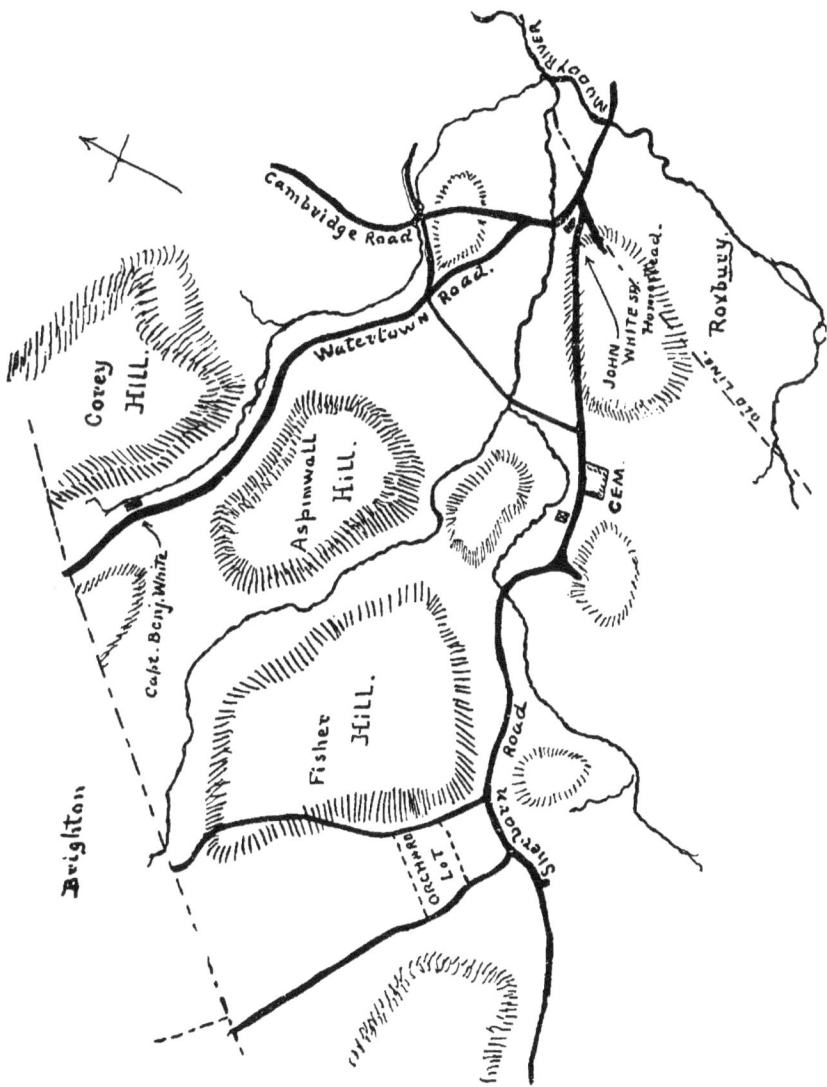

MUDDY RIVER

Cambridge Road

Watertown Road.

Corey HILL.

Aspinwall HILL.

Fisher HILL.

Capt. Benj. White.

Brighton

ORCHARD LOT

Sherburn Road

CEM.

JOHN WHITE sr. Homestead.

old line.

Roxbury.

In 1650, John White made his first purchase of land in Brookline, buying from Mr. Thomas Oliver 50 acres of upland, 18 acres of marsh and 6 acres of fresh marsh for £130, "to be paid for in good merchantable corn and fat cattle. "

His homestead was located very near the present Whyte's block and the engine-house, between Walnut and Washington streets. Portions of this land are yet in the possession of his descendants, having passed from one generation to another to the present time.

To this first estate John White added various tracts of land in different parts of the town, so that before his death he had become a considerable proprietor.

The gradual rise of local self-government in Muddy River can be readily traced in the volume printed by the town in 1875. Until 1685, the chief officers were the constable, the surveyors of the highways, and the perambulators of the bounds, with occasionally a tythingman, appointed from those living in the hamlet by the Selectmen of Boston. After the full meeting of the inhabitants of Muddy River held Jan. 19th, 1686, which accepted the order in council authorizing the hamlet to choose its own officers and meet its own expenses, there was a practically independent management of local affairs until 1705, when Brookline became a regularly incorporated town.

In 1654, John White, senior, with Peter Oliver, Peter Aspinwall and William Davis, is chosen to lay out the highway from Roxbury to Cambridge, through Muddy River.

In 1655 and 1666, he is chosen constable. For five years he was perambulator of the town bounds, and for four years one of the surveyors of the highways. His last service seems to have been in 1676, when, with Peter Aspinwall and Edward Devotion, senior, he is on a committee chosen by the Selectmen of Boston "to inspect and prevent excessive drinkage and such disorder in private and unlicenced houses of entertainment in Muddy River. "

Under date of Feb. 20, 1672, we find that "Liberty is granted to John White of Muddy river, Senr., to cutt five-oake and ffive maple trees of the comon at Muddy river; provided, he doe what he can to secure the rest from others or to give notice of any that shall offend in that kinde."

That the grievances of our townspeople over changes in the highways of the town are of ancient standing, is curiously shown by the following entries in the records, and the methods pursued in obtaining settlement suggest those sometimes employed by contending street-railway companies :—

28, 12, 1658. "Whereas a highway was laid outt att muddy river as by a record dated June 8 1658 through the land of Jno. White att Muddy River and so by Tho. Gardners to ye farme of Isaac Stedman, itt is hereby declared yt, ye said way, so laid out, shall be reputed ye townes highway and the other way in ye law is hereby relinquished. And itt shall bee lawful for ye said Jno. White either to fence out ye sd highway, or else, to sett up gates such as may bee easy for opening to travellers ; and if any leave ye sd gates open att any time they shall pay five shillings for every defect; being legally convicted thereof."

An entry about a month later shows the sequel and gives us a side-light upon the character of this early settler. It reads : 31, 1, 1659 "Upon information brought yt Jno. White at muddy river hath stopt up the highway yt was laid out through his fields with a stone wall; Itt is ordered yt ye Treasurer shall issue forth a warrant for a fine of twenty shillings, for his offence, to bee levied by distress by ye constable, and so from day to day twenty shillings till ye sd White open the way again."

We may safely presume that there was a "considerable discourse" over this matter and that the offending wall was removed, for in a few months a third entry records the conclusion as follows: 25. 12. 60. " Whereas a highway was laid outt through ye land of John White at muddy river whereby he pretends much damage ; Itt is therefor ordered yt his proportion of the ordinary rates to towne and country for ye next four years shall be allowed to him by the towne, which allowance is accepted by ye sd White for full satisfaction." This result may have encouraged the complaint lodged in 1667 against James Pemberton for setting up a gate in the highway by the bridge; but this complaint was adjudged to be groundless; "for as much as that for many years before, and some time sense John White's dwelling there a gate was erected and accepted in or near that same place."

There are various other references to John White in the town records, and the Suffolk Deeds contain several; among them, the testimony of John Gore, John Winchester and Joshua Kibby, about a case of disputed measurement of land near Corey Hill, very quaint in its language but too long to to be quoted.

In 1669 Edward Cartwright of Boston makes John White of Muddy River and Edward Morris of Roxbury trustees of his estate for the benefit of himself and his heirs.

In the same records for 1657 we find that John White witnessed an agreement made by Thomas and Elizabeth Wiswall of Newton, then called Cambridge Village, binding them to give to their son Enoch, in the event of his marriage, their three lots of land and two houses at Dorchester.

Thus encouraged, Enoch soon married Elizabeth, daughter of John Oliver of Boston, who for his character and attainments was called "The Scholar."

A granddaughter of this marriage became the wife of John White's grandson Edward, and it is of special interest for the clue it gives us to the origin of one of the persistent family names.

Enoch Wiswall and Elizbaeth Oliver had twelve children, and they gave the name of " Oliver " to one of their sons. A daughter of this Oliver Wiswall named one of her sons Oliver White, and each succeeding generation has had an Oliver among its sons. At the present time there are three of that name living.

Until there was a church established here in 1717, most people of Muddy River and Brookline went to the Roxbury church and its records are rich in references to them. In the list of "such as adjoyned themselves to the church at Roxbury " is the entry for " 1677, 2d month 29th day ; John White, Senior, of Muddy River, was received with good acceptance." Taken with what is recorded as to John White's services in his community and the usual close association of citizenship and church membership in the colonial days, the fact that he did not become a church member until he was sixty years of age is certainly interesting. It is not on record that he had previously " taken hold on ye covenant, " as the entries of half-way membership read, but we may suppose that he had done so. The incident of the stone wall in the highway indicates a man of determined character, while the advanced age of his coming into the church points to one not fully in accord with early theocratic ideals of civil government.

John White, Senior, died in 1691, and his widow, Frances, five years later. Probably their remains were buried at Eustis street in Roxbury. No monument to them can be found at present.

Their eldest son Lieutenant John White and his wife were buried there, and their headstones are as clear-cut as when new. Lieutenant John died about a year before his mother's death.

It is worth while to recall to our minds for a moment some of the stirring events filled with far-reaching meaning, which took place during the life-time of this early settler of our town.

As a lad he saw the accession of Charles I. and could recall it much as a man of fifty can now recall our Civil War.

When a young man he felt the political and ecclesiastical pessure which preceded the English Revolution, and he had been swept to New England on some wave of the great tide of Puritan emigration. In the days of the Long Parliament, of the War and of Cromwell, he was in Watertown, while the times of the Protectorate, the Restoration of Charles II., of James II. and the coming of William and Mary, were those of his living at Muddy River.

In New England he may or may not have seen the Pequod War, but he witnessed the efforts at unity of Church and State, the driving out of Baptists and of Quakers in pursuance of that policy, the establishment of the Half-way Covenant, designed to widen the suffrage, but which paved the way to the decline of theocratic rule. Then came the times of the

Narragansett War followed by the anxious days of Andros and, as his life draws to a close, the Witchcraft and the New Charter.

On April 13, 1691, two days before his death, he signed his will, which was witnessed by Joseph Griggs, Joshua Gardner and Roger Adams. It is on record in Suffolk Probate, and some of its items are of interest to us for their light on the times and the man.

"I give and bequeath to my grandson John, son of my eldest son John £40 in money or as money; my fowling-piece and my best silver wine-cup being part thereof. To my grandson Benjamin a carbine.

" To my granddaughter Mary; daughter of my son Joseph; my second-best wine-cup, being silver.

" To my grandchild Mary; daughter of my son John; a silver dram-cup. To my sons John, Joseph and Benjamin a whip-saw, hatchill and a great iron pot, to be equally between them. I give and bequeath to my sons John, Joseph and Benjamin a certain parcel of land containing 32 acres; acres his lot; excepting four or five acres thereof; which is elsewhere given to my son Joseph; to be by them planted with an orchard to be improved for their eldest sons, to bring them up in good learning and upon failure of sons to their eldest daughters, to be reserved against their marriage. . . And that what expense they shall be at in planting an orchard, or otherwise about the said land, shall be paid out of the income.

" And the said land shall always be kept in an orchard, by my sons or their heirs, which they shall keep clean from bushes. Further, I order that the aforesaid land shall be forthwith planted by my sons and their heirs, kept well pruned, and all dead trees supplied by living; a nursery being kept therein for that end.

" I further will that those who are brought up to learning be kept at the college seven years. "

Without having precisely located this interesting orchard it seems probable that it was not far from the land recently bought by the town on Reservoir Lane. We note that a few acres of the orchard lot had been given to Joseph White. In 1703 Joseph deeds this to Benjamin his son and describes it as part of the lot purchased of John Ackers by his late father John White. In 1714 Benjamin White describes it in the same way and as " lying undivided with the shares of his kinsmen. "

In 1716 Edward White of Brookline, Gentleman, and John White of Boston, Gentleman, sell to Benjamin White, Jr., of Brookline, husbandman, their one third parts of this orchard lot bounded southwesterly by a highway leading to Newton ; northwesterly by land of Peter Boyleston ; northeasterly by a highway leading to Cambridge line, and southeasterly partly by land of Benjamin White, Jr., and partly by land of Joseph Gardner. The provisions of this will give a vivid conception of the value put upon good learning in early days, but not for the young women.

It should be noted here that although the will was dated in 1691, it was probably written a good many years earlier, and it is probable that John White, Senior, had already divided his lands among his sons by deeds of gift. Excellent use was made of the improvement or income of the orchard.

The grandson John, who received the " best wine-cup and fowling-piece, " graduated at Harvard in 1685 and prepared for the ministry, taking two degrees. He combined scholarly tastes with a good capacity for business and for public affairs. Judge Samuel Sewall speaks most highly of him in his diary. He was chaplain to Sir William Phipps. For three years he was a representative from Boston in the Legislature and Clerk of that body for twenty years. In 1697 he was chosen Fellow of Harvard College, and in 1713 its Treasurer, acting as such from 1715 to his death. He was one of the trustees of the Province-Loan, and one of the twenty-two proprietors of Leicester, Mass. In 1721 he was inoculated for small-pox by Dr. Zabdiel Boylston, and died from complications ensuing during convalesence. He was never married.

The eldest son of Joseph White was Benjamin, Jr., as he was called, and afterward Deacon. For some reason his next brother John was put to learning in his stead, and, graduating at Harvard in 1698, entered the ministry, and in 1702 was settled at Gloucester, where he remained until his death in 1760. He married three times and had eleven children. Of his seven sons, two graduated at Harvard College.

Of the third grandson, Edward, son of Benjamin White, Senior, also a Harvard graduate, we shall speak later.

In the division of John White, Senior's, real estate in Brookline the share of the youngest son, Benjamin, included the homestead and adjacent lands with all buildings thereon and all other lands then in Benjamin's possession. Those about the homestead fronted along what is now Washington street, from the foot of Walnut street to the railway bridge, and extended westerly along both sides of Walnut street. The other lands were on upper Washington street near its junction with Beacon street, probably including what in later times we have known as the James Bartlett farm. This Benjamin White was born about 1646, and is usually referred to in town records as Senior, to distinguish him from his nephew, Deacon Benjamin White, Jr. He is also called Sergeant and Ensign White. He describes himself as "yeoman." In his younger days he probably carried on the "upper farm" near Corey Hill and, later, after the death of his father, made the homestead in the village his residence. He married about 1680. His wife Susanna is supposed to have been daughter of William and Susanna (Hawkes) Cogswell of Chebacco parish of Ipswich, though I believe this is sometimes questioned.

Benjamin White died in 1823, and his gravestones (head and foot) are in the old Brookline burying ground, one of the earliest to be found there. The inscription reads:—

Here lyes interred
ye body of Mr.
Benjamin White who
departed this life
January 9th day
172⅔
aged about seventy
seven years.

His widow survived him five years, but I find no memorial stone of her. Their son obtained leave of the town to build a tomb, and with one exception, there are no visible burial-ground monuments to any of this family in Brookline until we come to the tomb built by the late Oliver Whyte. The body of his father, Oliver, Senior, was removed from an old tomb and put in his new one. I have already stated that Lieutenant John White and his wife were buried in Roxbury. Joseph White and his wife Hannah were buried in Brookline and their headstones are well preserved.

Ensign Benjamin White served the town as perambulator of bounds in 1685-90-93; as surveyor of highways in 1694. He was selectmen for eight years. In 1707, with John Winchester, Senior, and Lieut. Thomas Gardner, he was assessor of the Province Tax. He was one of the petitioners for the incorporation of the town and he is on record as one of the committee of seven, appointed to treat with Mr. James Allen in 1717, to secure his services as minister of the parish church.

In seating the church, *i. e.,* assigning to each his or her place of sitting, a duty performed by a special committee of five, *viz.,* John Winchester, Sr., Thomas Gardner, Sr., Joseph White, Capt. Aspinwall and Thomas Stedman, Ensign Benjamin White was assigned "the seat or spot at the right hand of the coming in at the east door of the meeting-house, valued at three pounds." These pew-spots, when accepted by those designated by the committee at the prices attached, became the property of them and their heirs with the condition that, if any proprietor removed from the town or "became reduced to such mean circumstances as not to be able to pay his public taxes," then the title should revert to the town upon payment to the proprietor of the original price and the cost of building the pew. Proprietors built their own pews and pew-windows, the town keeping the latter in repair, and among other votes we read : "Voted that Captain Timothy Corey be granted liberty to cut a window in his pew at his own expense, provided he cut no braces, and that Mr. Moses White's window be moved as far as may be without being carried out of his pew."

Next to Ensign White sat his nephew, Dea. Benjamin White, Jr., with his family of four sons and three daughters, while next beyond, in the northeast corner, sat Peter Boylston with his six daughters and their brother, grandchildren of Ensign White. Peter Boylston, an elder brother of the famous Dr. Zabdiel, had married Ann, second daughter of Benjamin White, and in the row of girlish heads was the future mother of a President, for Susanna by her marriage with John Adams of Braintree became mother of President John Adams.

Mary White, third daughter of Benjamin, married, in 1710, Rev. Timothy Ruggles of Roxbury. He was a Harvard graduate of the class of 1707, and a month after their marriage he was ordained minister of Rochester, Mass., where his pastorate lasted fifty-eight years. Theolatia Ruggles, wife of Hon. Ginery Twichell, and Mr. Cyrus W. Ruggles, who so long kept the post-office in the old Brookline railway station, were among the descendants of this marriage.

Susanna, the fourth daughter, married Captain Robert Sharp, third of the name. She died in 1770 at the age of eighty, and the names of Robert Sharp Davis and Mary Sharp Clark tell of her descendants in various Brookline families.

Elizabeth, fifth daughter of Ensign White, married William Fairfield of Boston, and Joanna, the youngest daughter, married Joseph Ruggles of Roxbury, a brother of Rev. Timothy Ruggles, just mentioned.

Edward, the youngest beneficiary of the orchard, born in 1693, was the only son. Benjamin White did not leave a will, but instead he executed a deed of gift eight years before his death, having practically the same effect. In it he describes himself " yeoman " and gives to his well beloved son, Edward White of Brookline, " clerk," all his houses and lands, all his stock of creatures living and dead ; all tools and utensils of husbandry without doors ; his black servant (slaves were not at all unknown in 18th century Brookline), one jack, a copper, one pair of dogs, a spit and a pair of iron racks of his movables within doors. The daughters were to inherit the rest of his personal property. Edward was required to pay to each sister at the death of each parent, £25 to help provide their mourning. After the death of both parents he was to pay each married sister £100 and each unmarried sister £200, and the receipts for each of these payments are duly entered in the Suffolk Probate. Their father also reserved to the unmarried daughters the southerly end of his house, consisting of one upper and one lower room, with privilege of the cellar, also convenient diet and firewood.

After making the deed of gift Benjamin leased to his son Edward one half of all his houses and lands for £40 per year.

Edward, who had graduated at Harvard in 1712, was now twenty-five years of age and had just married Hannah, daughter of Oliver and Sarah (Baker) Wiswall of Dorchester. Where the young people made their new home cannot, perhaps, be ascertained. It may have been in one of the houses on the old lot at the Village, or, which is more probable, it may have been at the Bartlett farm, where, as Miss Wood tells us, he built the house taken down after the widening of Beacon street. Be that as it may, he brings into the family line a new and attractive figure.

We have seen John of Boston, the scholarly city man, and John of Gloucester, the lifelong minister. Edward of Brookline, youngest of the "orchard cousins," has also a liberal education, which he turns to the service of an enterprising man of business. He inherited a considerable estate from his father and he added to it several pieces of land aggregating about 75 acres. Most of it was near Corey Hill, on the northerly slope of Aspinwall Hill or bordering on Washington street. Other pieces were along the northerly side of Walnut street.

To his Brookline property he added tracts of land in New Hampshire, from the grants made by the Province to soldiers of the Narragansett War. Most of this land was in the Merrimac Valley opposite Manchester. References to these lands and to many events connected with the life of Edward White have been printed by the Historical Publication Society and need not be repeated. The town records from 1718 to 1761 show him to have been almost continuously in the service of the community, although at the first call he pays the town £5 to be excused from serving as its constable. He was chosen Moderator of a large fraction of the town meetings between 1719 and 1760. He was town clerk and treasurer for five years, while for nine years he was selectman and assessor. He was the town's representative in the Provincial Legislature for five years.

In 1721 the town chose him, with his cousin Samuel White and Robert Sharp, as trustee of the town's share in the Province Loan of £50,000.

He joined with John and Henry Winchester and Abraham Woodward in 1727 on a committee "to bring the schools into some good method" and the next year he was on another to locate the centre of the town for school purposes. That is the year when we find him in company with Thomas Cotton and Captain Gardner, charged with drafting an act to prevent geese from going upon the highways. 1728 found him on a committee to seat the meeting house, on another to audit the treasurer's accounts, another to carry on a lawsuit with some inhabitants of the south part of the town, and on another with Robert Sharp and Caleb Gardner to erect the North School.

A taste for military duties runs through this family. As we have seen, Benjamin, Senior, was called Sergeant and Ensign. In 1740 Edward White is entitled Captain, and in 1743 Major, while later each of his sons bore a minor title. A few years ago Captain C. P. Crawford of Milledgeville wrote me of an old commission preserved in the library of Emory College at Oxford, Ga. By the kindness of the college officers it was photographed and the plate sent to Brookline. It proved to be one issued in 1743 by Gov. Shirley appointing Edward White to be Major in the regiment of Colonel William Dudley and Captain of the Brookline foot company. The original had passed from eldest son to eldest son for four generations until given to Emory College by the widow of Judge Thomas Williams White of Milledgeville, who left no son to succeed him.

If we go into the old burying ground on Walnut street and pass along its central roadway to the large elm tree near its eastern end, we shall see on our left a little headstone of slate cut with small but clear letters, " Here lies ye body of Hannah White, daughter to Mr. Edward and Mrs. Hannah White. Died October ye 9th 1725, in ye 6th year of her age. "

Hannah was the first of the nine children born to Edward and Susanna White, and the little stone is the only visible monument excepting the one to Benjamin White, Senior, her grandfather, to any member of these families before the one erected by Oliver, great-grandson of Major Edward, near the southerly line of the grounds.

Of Susanna, the second child, only this is now known, that she was living and married in 1765, when her father wrote his will. She probably married Stephen Brewer of Roxbury. Hannah, born in 1728 and who died in 1800, married William Ackers of Brookline. Sarah, the next daughter, died unmarried.

John and Oliver each died unmarried in early manhood, consumption sweeping both away in 1771. The name of each appears once on the town meeting records, and each was an officer in the regiment of Colonel Francis Brinley. John was associated with his father in ownership of New Hampshire land.

Ann, the youngest daughter, married Col. James Wesson, one of the most active officers from Brookline in the Revolution, of whom extended notice is printed in the Publication Society's " Brookline in the Revolution. " She died of small-pox in 1776, contracted while feeding a tramp at her door.

Major Edward White died in 1769, his life having spanned almost the whole period of Provincial Massachusetts, the days of political and military training for the era of the Revolution. His widow outlived him eleven years.

By his will he gave to his son Benjamin, all of his lands on the northerly side of " the great country road leading from Watertown to Boston, " as Washington street was long called, with certain lots on the opposite side.

To his son John, he gave his mansion house with all lands adjoining and the buildings thereon, situated upon the northerly side of Sherborn road, and a piece of meadow opposite the mansion house on the northerly side of the Watertown road.

This shows that he was living at the village as early as 1765, and that his son Benjamin, was then living at the Bartlett farm. Other lands were divided to John and Oliver, the latter receiving his silver-hilted sword.

To his three daughters he gives his lands in New Hampshire, and among other property "his negro girl."

He specifies that his mulatto servant Cæsar is to wait upon his mistress so long as she shall live, and directs that neither Cæsar nor Primus shall be sold, but shall live with which of his sons he liked best but not living in idleness. From the First Parish records we learn that Primus died in 1770, while Cæsar died in 1792, aged eighty. Cuffy, who was deeded to Major White in 1735 by Leicester Grovenor, Esq., of Pomfret, Conn., for the sum of £80, had died in 1762.

To his widow he gave the use of one half of the mansion house, with such parts of the other buildings and of the garden as she might need, with all the poultry and the use of his household goods. Also one of his horses, which she liked best, and his riding-chair.

The sons were required to furnish their mother with six barrels of cider, nine bushels of Indian meal and four bushels of rye meal, with one hundred weight each of beef and of pork with fire-wood annually. Under the provisions of this will the shares of property given to John and to Oliver, passed by their deaths in 1771 to the eldest son Benjamin, thus left the only man in the family of the fourth generation. He was born in 1724 and had graduated at Harvard College in 1744, and at the age of thirty-two he had married Elizabeth, daughter of Thomas and Joanna (Gardner) Aspinwall, elder sister of Col. Thomas Aspinwall of the Revolution, and of Dr. William Aspinwall, the successor of Dr. Zabdiel Boylston. Like his father, he was a landed proprietor conducting business and farming and giving a great deal of time to the public service. He took a most active interest in the events leading up to the Revolutionary War, and during all its conduct was one of its earnest supporters. It seems somewhat strange that Miss Woods in her Sketches of Brookline should have entirely missed Captain Benjamin White and his grandfather Ensign Benjamin, since their names are so recurrent in the town records. She specifies in her notes on the family, that Major Edward was the son of John White, and that Mr. Oliver Whyte, our Town Clerk, whom she probably knew, was a son of Major Edward.

From 1762, Captain Benjamin White served the town as selectman and assessor for ten years. He was representative in the General Court for eleven years, receiving a vote of thanks from the town for this service and another for his services as treasurer.

In 1667 the town voted unanimously to take all prudent and legal measures to promote industry, economy and manufactures in the Province and to discourage the use of European Superfluities, and Captain White was on a committee with Samuel Aspinwall, William Hyslop, John Goddard and Isaac Gardner to draft a form of subscription against receiving these European Superfluities.

In 1768 he was chosen to meet the delegates of the several towns at Faneuil Hall. Upon the organizing of the committees of correspondence in 1772, Captain Benjamin White was one of the Brookline members, and he was the town's representative at the General Assembly at Salem in 1774, acting under a set of formal instructions drawn up by Dr. William Aspinwall, Major William Thompson and Mr. John Goddard. In 1776 he was given the title of "Honorable," the first instance of its use found in the town records, probably bestowed for his services as Councillor. He was many times Moderator of the town meetings and his last service was in 1783 as representative. He lived long enough to see the constitution ratified and the new government for which he had so earnestly worked, set in motion.

Aside from the record of his public political services there are some other interesting items preserved to us. He was one of the committee chosen to consult and report to the town as to the cost of a steeple for the meeting house, where in to hang the bell which was given in 1771 by Nicholas Boylston. This question greatly agitated the town. Upon receiving the report of the committee, it was voted to erect the steeple, specifying "that it is to be no higher than Dr. Boylston's steeple is." A later meeting voted to reconsider and, instead, to build only a tower with a proper roof. Motions to reconsider this vote were lost at two succeeding meetings. Meantime the town decided to build a porch at the east end of the meeting house, making Captain White, Squire Gardner and Mr. Isaac Child a committee to attend to it. The same meeting constituted Captain White, with Deacon Ebenezer Davis and Deacon Joseph White a committee to look after the tomb which Mrs. Mary Craft is given leave to build.

Before long the town decided to grant the spot in the meeting house where the women's stairs were, to Captain White, he agreeing to build and finish the porch at the east end, at his own expense, and to carry the women's stairs into it.

Finally, in June 1772, the town reconsidered its vote against building the spire, and appropriated £100 to pay for it, levying this tax against "the real and personal estates and faculty and non-residents."

In 1790, Captain Benjamin White died. His wife, Elizabeth Aspinwall, had died in 1785, and he had married in 1788, Esther Daggett, who survived him. His real estate in Brookline comprised over 220 acres, and among those concerned with the settlement of it are several closely connected with the times and the families we have reviewed. Ebenezer Davis, one of the administrators, and Benjamin Davis, one of the bondsmen, were cousins, their fathers being of the same names, and sons of Deacon Ebenezer Davis, a descendant by his mother and his grandmother from John White, Senior.

From Ebenezer descended, through his marriage with Lucy Sharp, Robert Sharp Davis and his brothers, General Phineas Stearns Davis and Samuel Craft Davis, the well known merchant of St. Louis.

Both Benjamin Davis and his father had been successful farmers for the Boston market, their farm occupying the space between the brook and Davis avenue, on the westerly side of Washington street, where later lived Benjamin Baker Davis, the last man of that branch of the Davis line. Among the appraisers were Squire Stephen Sharp and Mr. Joshua Boyleston, whose pictures Miss Woods has drawn for us so pleasantly.

Captain Benjamin and Mrs. Elizabeth White had five children, Susanna, born in 1756, Edward, 1758, Thomas, 1763, John, 1766, who died at the age of two years, and Oliver, born in 1771.

As each of the three sons who lived to maturity was married, the tracing of the family line is less simple than in the case of the preceding generations in which there was but one adult male member in each, to whom fell the family estate. Before taking up the story of the next generation let us notice what became of Mr. White's lands as they passed into the hands of those with whom they are associated in our own minds. Captain White died intestate, his son Thomas and Ebenezer Davis were administrators, and Thomas Aspinwall, John Goddard and Captain Timothy Corey made the division of the estate.

Under the terms of his father's will, the death of his two brothers made Captain Benjamin White the owner of all the lands in Brookline, bequeathed to his three sons by Major Edward. These lands lay along both sides of the Watertown road and bordered the Sherborn road on its southerly side from the Village to what is now Cypress street, then called the New Lane. There were also the customary portions of salt marsh near Charles River and the Back Bay, and of woodland in the southerly part of the town. In 1795, Thomas White sold to John Gardner fifty-one acres of land, bounded southerly by the Watertown road with the house thereon, also ten acres and the barn thereon, bounded northerly by the same road. In 1797 John Gardner sold the same lands to Timothy Corey.

In 1800, Timothy Corey sold to Elijah Corey, forty acres of the land on the north side of the road with the house, and in 1843, Elijah Corey sold the same tract of land and the house to James Bartlett, who held it until the general cutting up of the old farmsteads when the widening of Beacon street took place. The one hundred acres of land on the slopes of

Aspinwall Hill passed into the hands of Dr. William Aspinwall, brother of Mrs. White.

In 1794 Thomas White bought in the land bordering along the Sherborn road, and in the same year the wood-lot adjoining Jonathan Mason's land was sold to George Cabot.

In 1800 and in 1803, Thomas White sold to Oliver Whyte, described as a merchant of Petersburg, Georgia, the land from the corner of Village lane and Walnut street to the present Irving street.

In 1820, after the death of Thomas White, Oliver bought about twenty-five acres more of this land along Walnut street, of John Robinson, administrator of the estate of Thomas White.

The same year Henry Coleman bought about sixteen acres of this land from Oliver Whyte, and in 1822 sold part of it to Joseph Sewall, "being the southwest part of what is called Walnut Hill."

Other portions were bought by Samuel Philbrick and parts nearer the village by J. S. Wright. The easterly point of this land was retained by Mr. Oliver Whyte, where he built his mansion house, which stood there until the new portion of High street was opened. Certain lots of land in this vicinity are yet owned by his great-grandchildren, making continuous possession in this family for eight generations.

The children of Capt. Benjamin White were not baptized in infancy. In the First Parish record of baptisms under date of 1775, 4th Sept., we find the name of Susanna White, adult. Then in the marriage record under the same date we find the names of Nathaniel Seaver and Susanna White. The date of death entered on both these records establishes the identity of the bride. For this we are probably indebted to the painstaking care of Dr. Pierce. There is in town an excellent full-length portrait of this young couple painted soon after their marriage.

Mr. Seaver was of the Roxbury family descended from Robert Seaver in which the name Nathaniel occurs again and again to the present time. His father was the Nathaniel Seaver, Sr., who married first, Hannah, daughter of Deacon

House of Oliver Whyte, Senior.

Benjamin White and Margaret Weld and who married, second, Sarah Stevens, whose child Nathaniel, Jr., was.

The father's name appears frequently in the Town Records from 1723 to 1764, while that of the son appears but once, when in 1776 he served with Deacon Elisha Gardner and Captain Timothy Corey as a committee to sell at auction the pew of Mr. Isaac Winchester, deceased. Nathaniel Seaver, Jr., was half brother of Hannah, wife of Mr. John Goddard, and his name appears on the tablet in the Public Library presented to the town by that chapter of the D. A. R. which bears his sister's name.

Another half-sister, Mary Seaver, married David Ockington, *grandfa-* to whom we shall recur later.

Seven children were born to Mr. Seaver and Susanna White; of these three died in infancy and one was of unsound mind. Their second son, Benjamin Franklin Seaver, died unmarried when a young man while on a mercantile voyage to South America. Their youngest child, Susan White Seaver, became the second wife of Moses Grant of Boston, a name well known a generation ago. She died at Philadelphia while on a journey seeking relief from the attacks of consumption.

Before 1790, Mr. Seaver had become one of those merchants and shipowners whose enterprise, after the Revolution, was carrying the flag of the new Republic into ports all over the world. In April, 1792, on board his ship the "Commerce" of Boston, he sailed from Madras bound for Bombay. His eldest son, Nathaniel Seaver, third, a lad of sixteen, accompanied him, and the ship's first mate was David Ockington, *Jr. Son*
Mary before mentioned, also from Brookline. In the Arabian Sea adverse winds drove them far to the northwest, and they lost their reckoning so that while thinking they were on the Malabar coast, they were in fact midway the southern shore of Arabia off Cape Morebet. On the tenth of July the ship struck on a bar and the next day they were compelled to take to their boats. Muscat, about four hundred miles to the eastward, was their nearest port, and they had hopes of sailing thither. Their small boats, however, were unfit to withstand

the storms they encountered, and they were driven ashore. Their crew consisted of twenty white men and seventeen Lascar sailors. In the landing, one boat was swamped and young Seaver and two others were drowned. In this strait, being unprovided with arms, they were at once attacked by Arabs and stripped of everything, even to their clothes. They then began a march toward Muscat without food or raiment, under a burning sun, along a shore almost destitute of water. Their sufferings were dreadful, and in their distress they separated into small groups. So far as is known only eight of the seventeen whites reached Muscat after a month of travel. Mr. Seaver was one of those who perished, but David Ockington escaped and returned to Brookline, where he died in 1822 at the age of seventy-six. The details of this disastrous voyage may be found in a little leather-bound volume printed at Salem in 1794, entitled "Saunders Journal," by Daniel Saunders, one of the survivors.

Some time after the death of Mr. Seaver, his widow married, as his second wife, Samuel Gore, a descendant in the fifth generation of John Gore, one of Roxbury's earliest settlers. He was the eldest of a large family of which the youngest was Governor Christopher Gore, whose mansion and estate at Watertown is still perhaps the finest example of stately beauty within our borders.

Mr. Theodore Watson Gore has kindly furnished me the following notes from his manuscripts. "Samuel Gore was a painter. He lived at one time in Green street at the corner of Pitts Lane, afterwards at the head of Brattle street. He was one of those stout-hearted patriots who furnished the muscle of the Revolution, whilst Samuel Adams and James Otis furnished the brains. He was one of those who seized the two brass guns 'Hancock' and 'Adams' now in Bunker Hill Monument, and conveyed them from the gun-house in Tremont street to the American lines under the very eyes of the British. Long before the Revolution, as early as 1722, a free school was established in what is now Mason street, near the corner of West street. It was then on the boundary of the Common; the land now lying between having been sold off the Common. The school was called the South Writing School, and was the fourth in the town, and later was known as the Adams School. A gun-house stood at the corner of West street at the beginning of the Revolution, separated by a yard from the school house. In this gun-house were kept two brass three-pounders belonging to Captain Adin Paddock's Train. These pieces had been re-cast from two old guns sent by the Town of Boston to London for that purpose and had the arms of the province engraved upon them. They arrived in Boston in 1768, and were first used at the celebration of the King's birthday, June fourth, when a salute was fired in King street. Captain Paddock had expressed an intention of surrendering these guns to Governor Gage. The mechanics who composed this company resolved that it should not be so. The British General had begun to seize the military stores of the province and to disarm the inhabitants. Accordingly the persons engaged in the plot met in this school-room, and when the attention of the sentinel stationed at the door of the gun-house was taken off by roll-call, they crossed the yard, entered the building, and, removing the guns from their carriages, took them to the school-room where they were concealed in a box in which fuel was kept. The loss of the guns was soon discovered and search made from which the school-house did not escape. The master placed his lame foot on the box and it was not examined. Several of the boys were privy to the affair but made no sign.

" Beside the school-master and Samuel Gore, Abraham Holbrook, Nathaniel Balch, Moses Grant, Jeremiah Gridley and ———— Whiston were concerned in this coup-de-main. The guns remained a fortnight in the school-room, at the end of which time they were taken in a wheelbarrow at night to Whiston's blacksmith shop at the South End and deposited under the coal. From here they were taken to the American lines in a boat. The guns were in active service during the whole war.

. "The first Glass-Works in Boston were located in what is now Edinboro street. The company was established in 1787. The Legislature granted the company the exclusive right to manufacture for fifteen years, and exemption from taxes for five years. The workmen were relieved from military duty. The company erected at first a brick building conical in form, but this, proving too small, was taken down and replaced by a wooden building, one hundred feet long by sixty in breadth. After many embarrassments the company began the manufacture of glass in November, 1793. Samuel Gore was one of the originators of this enterprise, but the company failed to make the manufacture remunerative.

" A collection of the arms of New England families was made during the last century. The original manuscript is at present inaccessible, but there exists a very careful copy printed by Isaac Child, Esq., a gentleman well versed in the rules of Heraldry. This transcript may be accepted as entirely authentic. The earliest recorded coats are dated 1701 and 1703, the latest 1724. It seems highly probable that the dates refer to the times when the memoranda were made. Mr. Child's copy says, made by John Gore, but it is certain that an English Heraldic Manuscript which was preserved with the book had inscribed in it the name of Samuel Gore. Dr. Drake has also a bill dated 1783 from Samuel Gore to Governor John Hancock, in which these items occur : —

To painting chariot body and wheels. .	. £15-0-0
To painting sill of coach and wheels. .	. 1-4-0
To drawing arms on paper . . .	. 0-3-0

From this it would appear probable that Samuel Gore was the painter of the arms in the Manuscript.

" Samuel Gore was severely wounded in the affair of February 22, 1770. On that day some boys and children set up a large wooden head on a board faced with paper, on which were painted the figures of four of the importers who had violated the merchant's agreement (as to the paying of the stamp-tax). This board was set up in the street before Theophilus Lillie's door. Soon after it was set up, a famous importer, who lived but a few doors off, came along and endeavored to persuade a countryman to drive his cart against it, but that individual had no disposition to meddle. Not long after this the importer tried to get a man with a charcoal cart to break down the image, but he declined also. The importer became vexed at his ill success and the bystanders became amused, so he returned to his own house followed by numerous boys and others. As he was returning he passed Mr. Edward Proctor, Mr. Thomas Knox, and Captains Reodan and Skillings, at whom he cried, 'Perjury, Perjury.' Upon this angry and insulting language followed upon both sides ; missiles were thrown at the importer by the boys who, at length, compelled him to shut himself up in his house. Not satisfied with being safe there, he most unwisely undertook to revenge himself, which he did by firing a gun from two windows, severely wounding Samuel Gore, then twenty years of age, and mortally wounding another boy, Christopher Snider, about eleven years of age, who died the following evening. On the twentieth of April next, Richardson was tried for his life and brought in guilty of murder. Governor Hutchinson, however, refused to sign the warrant, viewing the case as clearly being one of justifiable homicide. After lying in prison two years, Richardson was, on application to the King, pardoned and set at liberty.

"Samuel Gore was also one of the men who made up the Boston Tea Party. The tradition is that it was he who watched outside and gave the Indian whoop which was the signal to rush to the wharf."

Samuel Gore died in 1831 ; Mrs. Susanna Seaver Gore in 1832. Their niece, who remembers their home in the later years of their life, tells me that it was on or near Tremont street, close by the present Roxbury Crossing.

Thomas White, born in 1763, was the third son of Captain Benjamin, and for many years was one of the picturesque characters of Brookline. His name appears first on the town records as one of the chainmen employed by Mr. Jonathan Kingsbury of Needham, who surveyed a number of estates in the town in 1781. In 1792, the January Town Meeting was held at his house. In 1806, he was on a committee, with Mr. Thomas Whalley and Mr. William Marshall, to audit the accounts of the committee which was building the new meeting-house. He was also chosen clerk of the market for that year. In 1811 he was surveyor of the highways for the second district which seems to have been his last public service.

Thomas White lived during much of his adult life on the old John White homestead lot where Whyte's Block now is, at the foot of Walnut street. Possibly the old house formed a part of the group of buildings gathered there which included the country store kept by White and Sumner and later by George Washington Stearns. No doubt the patrons found it very convenient to the Punch Bowl Tavern, which ranged its inviting length along the opposite side of the village street. Some of the deeds on record at Dedham, style Thomas White "Trader," others at a later date name him "Gentleman." Among his closest associates was Mr. Isaac Davis, a man about his own age, a son of Benjamin Davis, Sr., and a grandson of Deacon Ebenezer Davis and Sarah White. Mr. Davis occupied a farm on both sides of the old Roxbury road, taking in the land from the Ebenezer Crafts farm to that of Ebenezer Francis, and extending from Muddy River up on to the slopes of Parker Hill, where the quarries are now worked. Mr. Davis lived to the age of eighty-seven. He married the eldest and the youngest daughters of Aaron White, who went from Brookline to Roxbury, and the members of my father's family heard many stories of old-time days from "Uncle Davis," as he was usually called. Not a few of these tales related to the doings of himself and "Tom White," for both were ardent sportsmen noted for their skill with both rifle and fowling-piece. Turkey shootings were then much in vogue and these cronies often went together. The shootings were a specula-tion to the man who set up the turkeys as well as to those who paid twenty-five cents per shot, and if Tom White and Isaac Davis attended one together, there was usually small profit to the proprietor. They were sometimes barred out, it is said, where their skill was known, or limited as to the num-ber of shots they might make.

Neither of the sons of Capt. Benjamin White married early in life. As we have seen, their father left a large acreage of land at his death, but it was heavily incumbered and his sons had to make their own way, and no doubt it took a sturdy effort to retain so much of the family estate as Thomas White became possessed of. In 1803, when forty years of age, he married Rachel Thayer, daughter of Capt. Jedediah Thayer of Woburn, who had been an officer in the Continental Army through much of the War of Independence. He was of the Braintree Thayers, sprung from Thomas Thayer, freeman of Braintree in 1640. On her mother's side, Mrs. White was a descendant of Richard Thayer, a freeman of Boston in 1647, but who died at Braintree. One of her nephews was Gideon French Thayer, founder of the Chauncy Hall School, and previously teacher in a Brookline private school. We noticed that Susanna White was baptized on her wedding day. Thomas White, her brother, was baptized by Dr. Pierce on May 19, 1805, on the day when he brought his oldest child, Thomas, then three weeks old for the same ceremony.

Thomas White died in 1819. Mrs. White, who was twenty-one years his junior, died in 1850. They had six children ; two of them died in infancy. Their second son, also named Thomas, died in 1836, at the age of twenty-five and unmarried. Their daughter Rachel, died also unmarried in 1841.

Their second daughter, Elizabeth, married Mr. W. H. Perry of Sherborn, and after her death, the youngest daughter, Susanna, became Mr. Perry's second wife.

The Perry farm on the southerly slopes of Brush Hill in Sherborn was a noted one a half century ago, especially for its apples ; and it is still one of attractive appearance. On the crest of the hill about an acre of ground is yet owned by Mr. Perry's children, though devoted to the uses of the town, which has built a tower thereon from which the outlook is very wide.

The youngest son of Benjamin and Elizabeth White was Oliver. For reasons connected with business convenience, he wrote his surname "Whyte," to which form of spelling his descendants have adhered. With his name we seem to step out of a past age, of which the characters must be pictured from records too often scanty, into one with which not a few now living are familiar.

Born in 1771, he went when a young man to engage in business in Georgia, to which state his oldest brother had already gone to make his home. He settled in Petersburg, becoming a prosperous merchant, where he seems to have remained until about 1803. That he kept pretty closely in touch with his native town, and looked forward to returning thither, is evidenced by his several purchases of lands of the old White homestead farm, as we have already seen. At the March meeting of 1810, he was on the auditing committee, and on the one appointed to inspect the town's stock of arms, uniforms and ammunition; with him were Captains Joseph Jones and Joshua C. Clark. From that date to the time of his death, Mr. Whyte was continuously in the town's service in various capacities. He was chosen Selectman and Assessor in 1818, and annually thereafter until 1831. He was Town Treasurer from 1829 to 1838. In making their report for that year the Auditing Committee, Dr. Charles Wild, Dea. Elijah Corey and Mr. Ebenezer Heath close by saying: "We wish to express our opinion that the thanks of the town are especially due to Mr. Oliver Whyte, late Town Treasurer, for the faithful manner in which he has so long performed the duties which he has now relinquished. "

The Post Office was established in Brookline, March 3, 1829, and Mr. Oliver Whyte was appointed post-master, continuing as such until the close of the year 1842. In the Public Library is a small manuscript volume containing his copies of correspondence and accounts relating to the Post Office. Every page of this book is evidence of his accuracy and care, and of his taste for preserving exact records. His returns to the General Post Office were made quarterly. For the term from July 1st to October 1st, 1829, being the first full quarter of the Brookline Office, the total receipts of the office were $69.09¼. The pay of the post-master for that quarter was $24.04½, being thirty per cent of the letter postage and fifty per cent of the rates on newspapers. For the same quarter of 1842 the total receipts were $122.57.

In December, 1841, Mr. Whyte addressed a letter to the Post-Master General which is interesting from several points of view. It reads: "Brookline, Dec. — 1841. Sir. Your circular requiring names and certificates of sufficiency of sureties

OLIVER WHYTE, SENIOR,
[In his 72d year.]

was duly received. But, as I am about to resign my office, as soon after the conclusion of the present quarter as I can have a suitable successor recommended by those most interested in the good management of the office, and feeling myself equal to the responsibility for the present quarter, I have not been so prompt in my reply as I otherwise should have been. The sureties which I gave on entering the duties of the office have, I believe, both deceased some years since. But as I have held the office so long (perhaps there is no person in the United States now living who received a commission as post-master so early and continued it so many years and made more prompt quarterly returns and payments), I hope you will excuse my omission to return sureties for the present quarter. I shall feel sufficiently interested to see that the person recommended as my successor is equal to the responsibilities and duties of the office.

" My first appointment as post-master was at Petersburg, Georgia, soon after the establishment of a post-office there in 1793 or 94, from Timothy Pickering (when the list of post-offices in the United States was contained on one side of a small sheet of paper), and renewed by Joseph Habersham and continued by Gideon Granger. While holding this commission I removed from Georgia to this place, and when a post-office was established here I took the appointment which I have held from that time, and my quarterly account has been made out and the balance deposited or payment made agreeable to orders from the department by my own hands. The balance of the present quarter I shall pay over to Mr. McIntosh, the mail contractor, without further orders from the department. C. A. Wickliffe, P. M. Gen."

At the end of a letter to John A. Bryan, second Assistant Post-Master General, enclosing final accounts, November 11, 1842, this memorandum appears :

" This compleats, in all probability, my official duties with the post-office department, which was commenced in 1793 or 4 and which, I hope, has proved generally correct and acceptable. "

The public service, however, for which Mr. Whyte is oftenest recalled and in which he engaged the longest was that of

Town Clerk, the duties of which office he performed for twenty-seven years, from 1814 to 1842. Among the things which he at once set about doing as Town Clerk was the making of a transcript of the old first volume of Muddy River Records, which was falling into decay. His copy, thus made, forms Book No. 3 of the Town Records. As an adjunct to this book he put into tabular form the birth-lists of many of the older Brookline families, grouping the names of the children under those of their parents, a work which he was well fitted to do and one which has since proved exceedingly helpful.

In 1812, Mr. Whyte married Mrs. Elizabeth (Richardson) Grafton, and their home was made in the house which, as before stated, stood where the Union Building now is, at the junction of High and Walnut streets. In 1844, Mr. White died. Mrs. White survived him until 1871 in her ninety-second year. They had three sons, and their only daughter is still living among us at an advanced age. Of their sons, Edward Henry married Miss Eliza Trescott, but died in 1847 without issue.

Benjamin Franklin married Miss Ellen Jane Hall. He died in Medford in 1887, and his five children live in the neighborhood of Boston.

Oliver Whyte, Jr., married Miss Elizabeth Bullard. He died in Brookline in 1885, leaving one daughter. He served the town for many years upon the Water Board and as Selectman, as well as in other capacities.

The eldest son of Captain Benjamin White, born in 1758, was named Edward, after his grandfather. No records of his boyhood remain to us, but we can easily imagine the eager interest with which he listened to what was talked of around him and at his father's house in the days just before the Revolutionary War. In 1775 the only organized military company in Brookline was the one under Captain Thomas White. This Thomas White was a son of Sarah Aspinwall and thus a cousin of Elizabeth Aspinwall, Edward White's mother. He was son of Benjamin White and grandson of Dea. Benjamin White, Jr., before mentioned. This relation-

ship may in some degree account for our finding Edward
White, though not yet sixteen and a half years of age, enrolled
as a private in this company and returned as one who marched
on the Lexington Alarm and as in service twenty-three days.
We next find him recorded as Ensign in Captain Nahum
Ward's company of the Ninth Massachusetts Regiment in
the Continental Army, commanded by Colonel James Wesson.
Col. Wesson, we may recall, was Edward White's uncle by
his marriage in 1768 to Ann White.

The Massachusetts Archives contain upward of twenty
references to Edward White and those at Washington several
more, from which it appears that he was promoted to Lieutenant in the Ninth Regiment dating from March 6, 1778. He
was transferred, as was Col. Wesson, to the Eighth Massachusetts, and again to the Third, in which regiment he was
Lieutenant of the Light Infantry Company under Colonel
Michael Jackson, as shown by a roll dated October 5, 1783.
In a notice of his death in the Savannah Evening Ledger it
is stated that he held a major's commission in the Continental
Army, but if so, no record of it is yet found, though he was
certainly styled Major and is so recorded in the Public Records
of Savannah. I have thought it possible that his having in
possession the old colonial commission of his grandfather of
1742, may have had something to do with it, the names being
identical. That he was in Brookline after the Revolution is
indicated by his joining his father in signing a mortgage note
recorded in 1784 at Dedham, among Norfolk Deeds.

In 1785, he went to Savannah, Ga., where he lived for the
remainder of his life. He was clerk of the Court Ordinary of
Chatham county for a number of years (the Probate Court), and
in 1797, June 22d, was appointed Surveyor of the Port of
Savannah, which office he held for life. The City Records
contain the following remarks : " The deceased bore a Major's
commission in the Revolution and acquitted himself with honor.
He was a resident of the city for twenty-seven years, during
which he filled several important stations. He has left a widow
and four children and a good property. Died at and was buried
from his house. His funeral was attended by the Union
Society and the Volunteer Corps of Savannah. "

In the old Savannah Cemetery, now a part of Colonial Park, is his burial stone, inscribed, "Sacred to the memory of Major Edward White, an officer of the Revolutionary Army, who died January 9th, A. D. 1812, aged 54. "

In 1792, Major White married Mildred Scott Stubbs of, Louisville, Georgia. She died July 23, 1825, and was buried at Milledgeville. They had three sons and one daughter, one son dying in childhood. The daughter, Maria Susan White, born in 1805, married in 1825, Mr. Francis Vincent de Launay. Of their four sons and five daughters, eight lived to maturity, and their descendants are now a numerous company.

Thomas White, born in 1801, became a planter and removed to Alabama and later to Mississippi, where he died in 1867. He was twice married, and by his daughters left a number of descendants now living. Of his sons but one, William Lee White, lived to maturity and was killed in 1864, a minor officer in a Mississippi regiment.

Major Edward White's eldest son, born in 1793, received the name of Benjamin Aspinwall, associating the names of his grandparents. To him our Brookline was a familiar place as well as the home of his ancestry. He came to Roxbury to live with his aunt, Mrs. Gore, while preparing for college, and in 1811, he graduated from Harvard with a Master of Arts degree. In 1815, he graduated in medicine at the University of Pennsylvania. Two years later he married at Savannah Miss Jane Eleanor de Clensie, and in 1821, removed and established himself on a fine plantation near Milledgeville, where he became a very successful physician as well as planter. To his estate he gave the name of "Brookline" and so it is still called, although a fire, some years ago, destroyed his house upon it. Dr. White was held in the highest esteem personally, and as a physician. For twenty-five years he was annually chosen president of the State Board of Medical Examiners.

He was one of the pioneers in establishing the Hospital for the Insane at Milledgeville, which he served in several capacities. The Civil War found him in his sixty-ninth year, but he at once volunteered and he served actively throughout the war. A part of the time he was Surgeon-General of the

Georgia State troops. Dr. White died on the sixteenth of
April, 1866. The next day the following notice of his death
appeared in the Milledgeville "Federal Union:— "

[From The Federal Union (Milledgeville, Georgia), April 17th, 1866.]

DEATH OF DR. BENJ. A. WHITE.

Dr. Benj. A. White died at his residence in this city M on
day morning, April 16th 1866, in the 74th year of his age
Dr. White was born at Louisville, Jefferson County, Ga., and
was the son of Maj. White, of Savannah, a distinguished
soldier of the Revolutionary War. He was educated at Cambridge, Mass., and was a classmate of Edward Everett, and
Drs. Webster and Parkman of Boston. He was Surgeon
General of the State of Georgia, during the first year of the
late war, and was President of the Medical Examiners Board
of this State at the time of his death.

He has been a citizen of this county nearly a half century.
Highly educated and devoted to his profession, he became
very soon after his entrance upon the field of duty, distinguished
as a physician and surgeon, not only in the immediate circle
of his practice, but throughout the State. The death of no
man in the community could be more regretted. Honest,
conscientious, highly gifted by nature, eminent in his profession, kind and affable in his deportment to all, he was the idol
of his family, beloved by his friends, and universally respected.
He died at a good old age, after a life of ceaseless labor, and
great usefulness, unspotted by an act of intentional injustice
to his fellow-man. Few men were more modest — but no
man was more decided when duty called upon him to act.

In contemplating his character, we are reminded of the
language of a distinguished author: " In life we shall find many
men that are great, and some men that are good, but very few
men that are both great and good. " Dr. White was both
great and good.

In this brief notice, we could not hope to do justice to the
life and character of such a man as Dr. White — other pens
must perform the office. He died surrounded by his wife,
children, relatives and friends, peacefully, rational to the last,
and with a clear and unobscured vision of his spirit's happy
home.

In his will he expressly provided that the merest essentials
should be furnished for his burial, and that a sum equivalent
to the customary funeral expense of a well-to-do gentleman,
should be given for the use of the orphans of Confederate
soldiers in his native state. This was done as he desired, but
the affection of his friends found expression in a wealth of

flowers which covered everything with their beauty. Mrs. White died November 17, 1873, and was buried in the family lot in the Milledgeville City Cemetery.

Dr. and Mrs. White had ten children ; of these, eight were married, and there were, all told, fifty grandchildren, so that this branch of John White's descendents seems in little danger of extinction or of the loss of the family name.

Dr. White's second son was named Thomas Williams, in memory of the Mr. Williams who had brought up Mrs. White after the early death of her parents. After preparing for college he came North, spending some six years before going home. He was one year at the Military Academy at West Point. Later he entered Norwich University at Northfield, Vermont, where he graduated in 1841. He also made an extended visit in Brookline with Mr. Oliver Whyte and his family. Subsequently he taught school in Ohio and then returned to Milledgeville, where he studied law and began the practice of that profession.

In 1849 he organized and led a company which, after eight months of hardships, made the overland journey to California. Mr. White was the engineer who laid out San José for the proprietors, and was chosen Mayor of the new city. He was also made judge in the county courts. In 1854 he returned to Milledgeville, having prospered in California ; and the next year he again visited Brookline. At the beginning of the Civil War he raised a company, of which he was captain for a year, when he was transferred to the Engineer Corps and put in charge of the coast works of Georgia. He planned and built Ft. McAllister, near Savannah, having command there when captured by Gen. Sherman in December 1864. Upon his release from Ft. Delaware, at the close of the war, he resumed the practice of law in Milledgeville, and was a county judge there also.

In 1866 he married Miss Henrietta Alston Kenan, leaving, at his death twelve years later, his widow and one daughter.

Dr. White's third son received the name of Samuel Gore ; he died when young, and the fourth son, born in 1824, took the name. In 1845 he graduated in medicine from Jefferson

Medical College at Philadelphia. His high standing is shown
by his having filled the position of demonstrator in anatomy
during a part of his last term. In 1846 he was appointed
assistant surgeon, U. S. Navy, remaining in this service until
the close of the Mexican War. He then settled in Milledgeville, where he practiced medicine until 1859, when he went to
Europe for travel and further study.

Returning on the outbreak of war, he was commissioned surgeon in Cobb's Legion of Georgia Cavalry, in which service he
continued four years. Dr. White was one of the ablest
surgeons in the army, and performed with great skill many
capital operations. He was a chivalrous and skillful officer,
greatly loved by his soldiers.

At the close of the war he returned to his native city, worn
down by service and with property swept away in the tide of
conflict. He again took up his profession until his death in
May, 1877.

For twenty years he was president of the Board of Trustees
of the Hospital for Insane, and held other offices of trust.
He was a ruling elder in the Presbyterian Church and a man
honored in the community where he lived. In 1849 he
married Miss Caroline Anne, daughter of Charles and Eliza
Bullock, their family numbering eleven children.

The fifth son of Dr. B. A. White was named Edward James,
as had been the eldest son who died in childhood. He was
trained as a pharmacist. In the Civil War he was commissioned Lieutenant-Colonel of Georgia State Militia, serving the
full four years. For several years he was treasurer and
steward of the Georgia State Sanitarium. He was twice married,
in 1852 to Miss Joseph J. Cotton, who left one son, Howard.
In 1858 he married Miss Melissa Adrian Hill, by whom he had
two sons, Joseph Hill and Thomas Edward. He died in 1881.

Mary Virginia was the eldest of Dr. White's three daughters.
In 1853 she married Rev. Habersham Jackson Adams of
Athens, Ga. She died the year following, leaving no children.

The next son received his father's name, Benjamin Aspinwall. He was born in 1835, and in 1861 he became Captain of
Company A, in Colonel Stiles' Twenty-sixth Georgia Regiment,
serving during the entire war. Subsequently he was employed

by his State in map-drafting. At a later period he engaged in farming. His home is at Marietta, Georgia.

He married in 1859 Miss Ella Aurelia Kenan, a sister of Mrs. Thomas Williams White. Mrs. B. A. White died in 1895, seven of her eight children surviving her.

Two daughters came next in Dr. White's family, Rosa Jane and Susan Elizabeth. Each was married in 1859, the first to Mr. James Augustus Clendenin, having a family of ten ; the second to Mr. Miller Bond Grant, having nine children, of whom six survived her.

I have been told that at the time of her marriage in 1817 Mrs. Benj. A. White was called the most beautiful girl in Savannah, and that her sweetness and beauty of character were equally pronounced. That the three daughters inherited the attractiveness of their mother, I am assured by their sister-in-law as well as by their friends in our Brookline, whom they visited a short while before their marriage.

The youngest of this numerous family, born in 1844, was given the much used name of Oliver. At an age almost the same as that of his grandfather at the opening of the Revolution, he enlisted as a private in 1861, serving in Company A, of Hampton's Cavalry, Young's Brigade, Phillips Legion in the Army of Northern Virginia.

In 1867 he married Miss Mary K. Johnston, a daughter of Colonel Mark Johnston. They have a family of seven children. Mr. Oliver White lives on the old home place, " Brookline," near Milledgeville. Not many now remember it as it was, filled with the young life of Dr. White's large family and their friends. The inevitable changes of more than two score years were vastly increased by the destruction and overthrow of the Civil War which claimed the father and the five sons, though their lives were spared. Mrs. Thomas W. White in a letter says : " You speak of returning to Brookline ; the name recalls many sweet memories of the 'Long ago' when we (young people then) had merry times at ' Old Brookline,' as father's country place was called. I wish you could have visited our family then. You would have been a welcome guest. Hospitality only expresses the life of it. The terrible changes since those happy days makes us fully realize the shortness of this life's joys."